SCHOLASTIC

News

Nonfiction Readers

Christopher Columbus

by
Lisa Wade McCormick

SCHOLASTIC INC.

New York Toronto London Auckland Sydney
Mexico City New Delhi Hong Kong Buenos Aires

These content vocabulary word builders
are for grades 1-2.

Consultant:
Richard W. Slatta
Professor of History
North Carolina State University

Photo Credits:

Photographs © 2005: Art Resource, NY/Vanni: 19, 21 top; Corbis Images: 1, 17, 21 bottom (D. K. Bonatti/Historical Picture Archive), 23 bottom left (Macduff Everton), 23 top left (Charles Michael Murray), 4 bottom left, 7, 20 top left (Jose Roldan/Archivo Iconografico, S.A.), 4 bottom right, 23 top right (Royalty-Free); Getty Images/Hulton Archive: 2, 5 bottom left, 13, 20 bottom (Kean Collection), 5 top right, 12; North Wind Picture Archives: 5 bottom right, 8, 23 bottom right (Nancy Carter), back cover; Stock Montage, Inc.: 20 top right; Superstock, Inc./Antonio Cabral Bejarano: 11; The Art Archive/Picture Desk/Dagli Orti/Museum of Modern Art Mexico: cover.

Book Design: Simonsays Design!

ISBN 0-516-23474-9

12 11 10 9 8 7 6 5 4 3 2 1   5 6 7 8 9 10/0

Printed in the U.S.A.   08

First Scholastic paperback printing, October 2005

CONTENTS

WORD HUNT

Look for these words as you read. They will be in **bold**.

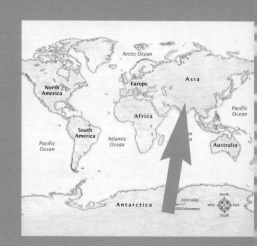

Asia
(**ay**-zhuh)

explorer
(ek-**splor**-uhr)

jewel
(jool)

4

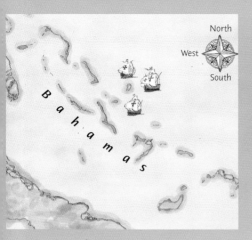

The Bahamas
(thuh bah-**ha**-muhz)

compass
(**kuhm**-puhss)

ship
(ship)

spices
(spissez)

Meet Christopher Columbus

Do you like going on adventures?

Christopher Columbus did.

He was a famous **explorer**.

Christopher was born in 1451, in Genoa, Italy.

He was the first person to sail from Spain across the Atlantic Ocean.

This is a painting of Christopher Columbus.

Christopher was a sailor.

He believed that he had found a fast, new way to reach **Asia**.

He would sail west across the Atlantic Ocean.

Christopher wanted **spices**, **jewels**, and other treasures from Asia.

spices

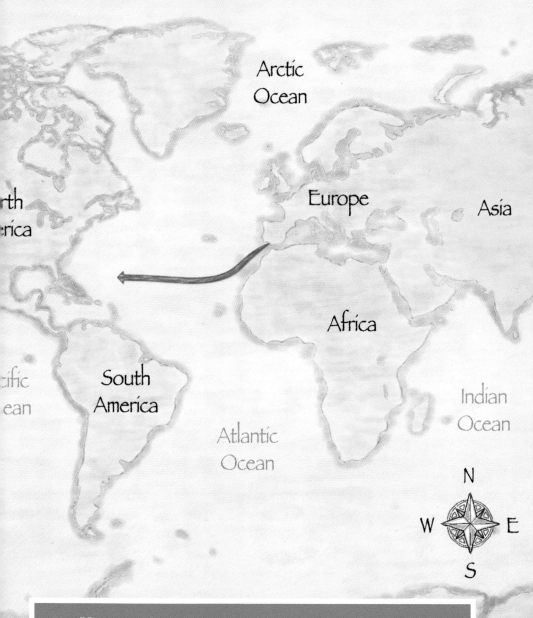

Arctic
Ocean

Europe

Asia

rth
erica

Africa

cific
ean

South
America

Indian
Ocean

Atlantic
Ocean

N

W   E

S

**Follow the red arrow. Columbus
sailed west to go to Asia.**

The king and queen of Spain gave Christopher money to pay for his trip.

Christopher used the money to buy supplies.

He started his trip on August 3, 1492.

Columbus started his trip in Palos, Spain.

Christopher had three **ships**.

They were the *Niña*, *Pinta*, and the *Santa María*.

Christopher used maps, a **compass**, and patterns in the stars to guide him.

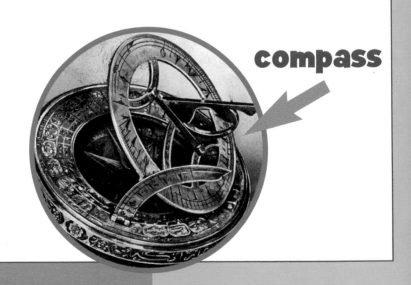

compass

13

His trip took 71 days.

Christopher reached the **Bahamas** on October 12, 1492.

The Bahamas are islands southeast of North America.

No one from Spain had been there before.

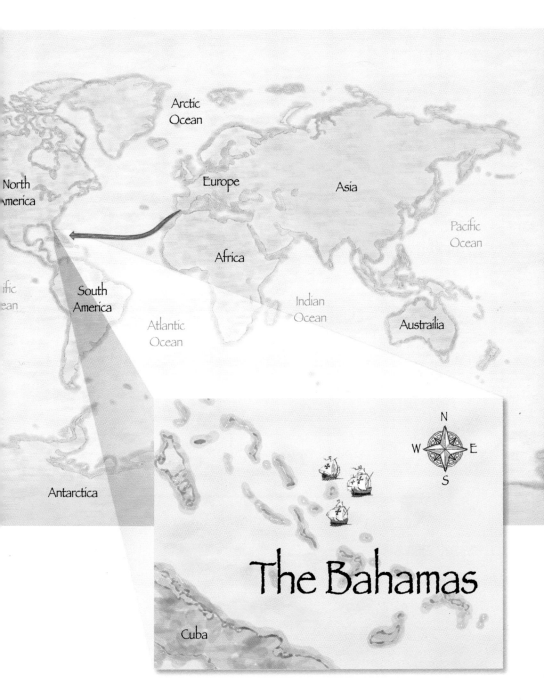

The Bahamas

Christopher thought he sailed to the Indies.

He called the people he met there Indians.

Christopher made three more trips to this new world.

He died on May 20, 1506.

This statue of Christopher is in Genoa, Italy.

Christopher the Explorer

1 Christopher Columbus is born in 1451.

2 In 1492, the king and quee of Spain give Christopher money for his trip to Asia.

3 On August 3, 1492, Christopher and his three ships sail west from Spain

5 Christopher makes three more trips to the new world between 1493 - 1504. He dies in Spain on May 20, 1506. This is a statue of him.

4 Land! On October 12, 1492, Christopher reaches the Bahamas. He meets people there and calls them Indians.

YOUR NEW WORDS

Asia (**ay**-zhuh) the largest continent on Earth

The Bahamas (thuh bah-**ha**-muhz) a group of islands southeast of North America

compass (**kuhm**-puhss) a tool that helps you find which direction you are going

explorer (ek-**splor**-uhr) a person who goes to places no one has been

jewel (jool) a special stone

ship (ship) a large boat that can travel in the ocean

spices (spissez) things that are used to make food taste better

What Treasures Did Christopher Hope to Find?

Gold!

Jewels!

Silk!

Spices!

23

INDEX

FIND OUT MORE
Book:
Christopher Columbus by Susan Bivin Aller.
(Lerner Publication Company, 2003)

Website:
http://www.imahero.com/herohistory/christopher_herohistory.htm

MEET THE AUTHOR
Lisa Wade McCormick tries to make every day an
adventure for her husband, Dave, and their two children,
Wade and Madison. Lisa is an award-winning reporter and
television producer. She lives in Kansas City, Missouri.